Original title:
Barking Up the Write Tree

Copyright © 2025 Creative Arts Management OÜ
All rights reserved.

Author: Wyatt Kensington
ISBN HARDBACK: 978-1-80567-237-1
ISBN PAPERBACK: 978-1-80567-536-5

Penned Within the Pair of Paws

A pup with pen, oh what a sight,
He scribbles words from morn till night.
His tail wags fast, ideas flow,
As recipes for treats begin to grow.

With every bark, a line appears,
In a world where laughter clears.
He writes of bones, of sunlit days,
His playful prose in silly ways.

Imagination in the Glen

In a glen where squirrels play,
A pup dreams big, in a funny way.
He imagines cheese and flying bones,
Whiskers twitch as he wildly groans.

A cat in shades, a wise old sage,
Chasing fluttering leaves off the page.
Together they weave, in giggly delight,
A tale of mischief that takes off in flight.

The Woof of Wisdom

A sage in fur, with poise and grace,
He offers wisdom in a happy place.
"Chase your dreams," he barks with glee,
"Just watch out for that pesky bee!"

With every woof, he delivers a pun,
A tail-twitching lesson that's just pure fun.
His students gather, all ears they perk,
Learning from the joyful quirks.

A Symphony of Sniffs

In the park where fragrances blend,
A furry maestro does not pretend.
He sniffs the air, composing a score,
Of treats and tails, a playful lore.

With every whiff, a giggle released,
A scruffy pup finds joy in the feast.
He conducts the breeze, a comedic show,
As laughter echoes, a happy flow.

Verse from the Field

In a field of scribbles, dogs run free,
Chasing words like squirrels, oh what glee!
With paws on paper, they leave their mark,
A draft so wild, it lights a spark.

Tails wagging tales, they spin and twirl,
As shadows of poodles begin to whirl.
They howl at the moon, then chase their dreams,
In flight of fancy, or so it seems.

A Sniff of Inspiration

A sniff of paper, a whiff of ink,
The pups ponder life, now what do you think?
They pause for laughter, paws on their snouts,
While plotting their plots with playful shouts.

A chuckle rises from the grass below,
As a beagle's tale becomes quite the show!
With every bark, a story grows,
In the world of whimsy, anything goes!

The Muzzle of Imagination

A muzzle of dreams, where whims take flight,
Chasing after treats on a starry night.
Each bark a chorus, a tune so bright,
In the dog's great tale, everything's right.

They scribble in sand, with tails held high,
Imagination soars, like birds in the sky.
A woof here, a wiggle, ideas galore,
Each tale they spin opens the door.

Tales from the Tail End

At the tail end of stories, laughter does swirl,
With pups weaving yarns, their antics unfurl.
From chasing their tails to rolling in grass,
Each moment's a gem, none can surpass.

With wagging enthusiasm, they bark out glee,
In the circus of life, they bring the spree.
Oh, the mischief they make, the joy they impart,
As tales from the tail end dance from the heart.

The Storyteller's Sylvan Retreat

In a grove where tales take flight,
The squirrels debate who's wrong or right.
With acorns as props, they spin their yarns,
While raccoons juggle under leafy barns.

A fox recites with a knowing glance,
The ants dance about, eager to prance.
The trees lean close, they want to hear,
As laughter echoes, dispelling fear.

The Playful Poet's Paradise

A rabbit hops with a pen in paw,
Sketching dreams beneath a straw.
The daisies chuckle, swaying blooms,
In this bucolic realm where whimsy looms.

Ode to the pie that no one made,
A llama laughs, while frolics invade.
With paper-kite clouds and sunny zest,
These joy-filled scribes sure know the best.

Howlings in the Whispering Woods

Wolves compose in moonlit nights,
Amidst the trees, their howls take flights.
With verses shared 'round campfire glow,
They trade puns like pros, stealing the show.

A fox chimes in, "I'm quite the bard!"
His tales of mischief leave them charred.
With echoes of laughter and silly glee,
These woodland bards write their legacy.

The Canine's Creative Confessions

A pup with dreams of becoming a star,
Pens his thoughts with a squeaky toy guitar.
His ballads of treats and mischievous schemes,
Bring giggles and gasps, fueling his dreams.

With a tilt of his head, he seeks applause,
From frogs in the pond, and even the jaws,
Of the cat who rolls eyes, yet can't resist,
The charm of a dog with a poet's twist.

Paws on the Pages

A pup with a pen seeks a rhyme,
Chasing shadows, lost in time.
With wagging tail, he scribbles away,
Tripping on words that come out to play.

He chews on a book and flips every page,
Each bark, a laugh, a comical stage.
With every scratch, a story unfolds,
A tail-wagging saga, brave and bold.

Echoes of the Literary Leash

Around the park, the lyrics flow,
His leash, a tether to tales we know.
Each step a stanza; he hops and prances,
Marking his territory, taking his chances.

In puddles of ink, he takes a leap,
Dropping ideas that make us all weep.
His playful barks echo through the trees,
A furry poet, bringing us to our knees.

The Poetic Pooch's Journey

With paws of prose and a nose for rhymes,
He wanders the world, lost in good times.
Every sniff sparks a metaphor bright,
Chasing the sun, under the moonlight.

His tales of biscuits and adventures grand,
Spread joy like treats from a gentle hand.
With each little bark, he crafts a new line,
A pup on a quest, so utterly fine.

Tails of Unwritten Tales

In a garden of verses, he sniffs for inspiration,
Each flower a word, a wild sensation.
With giggles and grins, his stories unwind,
A comic relief, to all of mankind.

He gathers his thoughts like sticks in a heap,
Summoning laughter, not one bit cheap.
For every lost ball, a tale will arise,
In the land of the silly, where humor flies.

Whispers of the Inked Canopy

In a forest of paper, ideas take flight,
Barking with laughter, the scribes write at night.
With pencils like wands, they conjure up dreams,
As ink spills like laughter in whimsical streams.

Frogs in the margins, they croak out a rhyme,
While squirrels with their acorns compose every line.
The trees listen closely, their leaves start to sway,
As the scribes share their secrets, come out to play.

Scribbles Under the Starlit Canopy

Under the twinkling, stars wink and twirl,
The scribblers gather, with ink all a-whirl.
They doodle and giggle, their pages a mess,
Creating wild tales, just for fun, no stress.

A raccoon in glasses critiques every word,
While owls offer wisdom, their thoughts rarely heard.
With snacks on their laps and imaginations grand,
They sketch out a story, a whimsical band.

Tails of the Textual Forest

In the textual woods, where the characters roam,
Cats tell their tales, while the dogs write at home.
Each bark and each meow, a chorus of cheer,
As the author pets plots, drawing characters near.

With tales of adventure, they leap off the page,
A dance of the sentences, a literary stage.
The forest alive with both puns and delights,
In this whimsical world, where the ink sparkles bright.

Paws Patrolling Pages

Paws patrolling pages, with purpose they stride,
While the ink spills like dreams, far and wide.
Little critters gather, all eager to hear,
The stories that bubble up, bursting with cheer.

With tails wagging stories and paws in the mix,
The scribbles of laughter come quick with each fix.
Fluffy muses ponder, their thoughts take a spin,
In this raucous world, let the fun times begin!

Leaves that Tell Stories

In the park, leaves dance and play,
Twisting tales of a sunny day.
Squirrels chatter with a flick of their tails,
While dogs chase dreams and wagging trails.

The grass whispers secrets, oh so absurd,
Of a lost sandwich or a wayward bird.
Each fallen leaf, a page to unfold,
In the library of nature, stories told.

With every rustle, they giggle and sigh,
As pups do pirouettes, reaching for the sky.
A beagle snorts at a tree's wise old bark,
While golden retrievers retrieve words from the dark.

And when the sun sets, casting shadows long,
Leaves gather round to weave their sweet song.
"Tell us your wishes, your dreams, and your schemes,"
Their laughter erupts like the wildest of dreams.

Ode to the Overnight Wanderer

Oh, the night's a cloak for the curious hound,
On soft, silent paws, mischief is found.
With noses that twitch and sparks in their eyes,
They embark on adventures where wonder lies.

Through gardens and fences, under the moon's glow,
Dodging the fetch games of exhausted and slow.
A chase after raccoons, elusive and sly,
While stars giggle loudly, "Oh look, it flew by!"

In shadows they scurry, with barks of delight,
As crickets serenade their whimsical flight.
Every squeaky toy is a treasure to find,
In the playful realm of a wanderer's mind.

And just as dawn breaks, unveiling the jest,
Those once-great escapades bring a warm nest.
So sleep, little traveler, 'neath sunrays that beam,
For the morning may call, but tonight was a dream!

Pondering in the Paws

What's the meaning of life, asks the wise old hound,
As he gazes at squirrels, both proud and profound.
"Is it belly rubs, or is it the treats?
Or sunbeams to lounge on while napping, oh sweets?"

By the fence, he ponders, with an ear twitching high,
As the mailman approaches, with a raised eyebrow.
"Should I bark for attention or lay low and wait?
Does wisdom reside in who's guarding the gate?"

With each squirrel that scampers, he scribbles in thought,
The philosophy of paws, a puzzle unsought.
A wag is a word, a roll is a tale,
In the book of the barker, there's never a fail.

So, here's to the thinkers, the loungers, the bold,
Who ponder in silence, with stories untold.
While each fluffy epiphany leaves a big pause,
Only to be answered with a twitch of their paws.

Canine Wisdom in Verses

In a world that spins with a tail-wagging spin,
What dogs know, oh my, where do I begin?
Every woof is a chapter, a bark is a rhyme,
In the canine ballads, there's never a time.

From the leash of the joy that runs freely and wild,
To the games with the shadows that each dog has filed.
They say that a nap is a lesson in grace,
And a mud puddle bath is a joyous embrace.

Oh, to chase down a feather, the thrill in the chase,
Is wisdom disguised with a woof and a race.
For every missing sock, there's a story that cheers,
With laughter that echoes through the bark of the years.

So gather round, humans, heed these wise pups,
For life is a treat, overflowing our cups.
With each joyous romp and wagging parade,
The humor of dogs is the best serenade.

The Literary Trailblazer

With pen in paw and whimsy bright,
A dog confounds the stars at night.
He scribbles tales of bones and treats,
While chasing squirrels on tiny feet.

Around the park, he dashes fast,
In search of stories meant to last.
He howls in verse, a poet's song,
Each wag a note where laughs belong.

His bark is clear, his prose a joy,
Comedic fluffs, not just a ploy.
With every woof, a pun takes flight,
Who knew that pups could write this bright?

So raise a toast to fur and fun,
This literary dog has just begun.
With every word, a giggle flows,
In canine tales where humor grows.

Fables of the Furry Muse

A cat in glasses writes with flair,
About the mice that dance and dare.
With every stroke, a giggle spills,
As tails entwine through funny thrills.

The dog, intrigued, begins to bark,
He scribbles on with a bright spark.
The tales unfold of muddy paws,
And silly squirrels who love to pause.

In fables thick with furry schemes,
The critters plot and craft their dreams.
With paws in ink and hearts so bold,
They share their yarns, a sight to behold!

And so they laugh, those furry friends,
In binding tales that never ends.
With every turn of page and bark,
They celebrate the funny spark.

Words Woven in Wilderness

In the woods where whispers twine,
A fox writes tales, both sharp and fine.
His quill a twig, his ink a stream,
He bursts with laughter, a writer's dream.

The bear comes by with honey snacks,
As squirrels offer puns in packs.
With every line, a jest erupts,
In nature's prose, the laughter leaps.

Amidst the trees, the stories grow,
Of mischief, games, and scuffles slow.
Each bark and chirp a rhyming scheme,
As wildlings dance in a merry dream.

So let them write beneath the bough,
With giggles shared, they take a bow.
In furry tales of wild delight,
They pen the world in laughter's light.

Under the Canopies of Inspiration

Under trees where shadows play,
The critters gather, bright and gay.
With whispers soft, they plot and scheme,
In a whimsical world that makes them beam.

A rabbit hops with tales to share,
While birds chirp sonnets of the air.
The world is a canvas, bright and wide,
With laughter echoing far and wide.

In every nook, a story hides,
Where silly antics and wit collide.
With each new page, a cheerful twist,
They craft a world that can't be missed.

So pause a while, enjoy the show,
In nature's book, let humor grow.
Together they weave, a vibrant thread,
Under canopies where fun is fed.

Scribbling Shadows of the Forest

In the woods where thoughts run free,
Squirrels write in harmony.
With nuts for ink and leaves for pages,
They craft their tales through all the stages.

A rabbit hops, he adds a line,
While birds compose, oh so divine!
The trees lean in, they want to hear,
What silly stories will appear.

One bark, one chortle, it's pure delight,
As shadows scribble, lost in the night.
The moonlight giggles, twinkles and shines,
These woodland tales are true gold mines.

Sentences in the Shade

Under branches, where cool winds play,
Words are woven in a playful way.
The sunbeams whisper, and giggles grow,
With each new sentence, more laughs to sow.

A turtle types with a snail as guide,
The pace is slow, but the humor won't hide.
Silly commas dance, and periods twirl,
In this forest of lines, imagination's a whirl.

As shadows stretch and daylight fades,
The critters gather for story parades.
Each giggle lifts like a leaf on high,
In this jolly shade, watch creativity fly.

A Bark and a Quill Harmony

With a quill in paw and a tail that wags,
The puppy barks while the kitten drags.
Together they pen a rhythmic rhyme,
Chasing each other, having a good time.

The forest echoes with laughter and glee,
As they write tales of a grand old tree.
In every bark, there's a punchline made,
With quills that dance in a playful parade.

One story says the moon's a pie,
And all the stars are sprinkles up high.
As they giggle and scribble in furry delight,
Their friendship grows strong, a marvelous sight.

Prose from the Paws

Paw prints trace a story bold,
Each plot twist comes with secrets untold.
With whiskers twitching and tails all about,
They weave their prose, no room for doubt.

The hedgehog's wisdom brings chuckles and snorts,
While ducks compose hilarious retorts.
In this wild tale, laughter's the theme,
As every character bursts at the seam.

Each chapter's a romp, a tumble, a cheer,
With paws and claws, they write without fear.
So here's to the stories spun under the sky,
Where critters at play, let their imaginations fly.

The Whispers from the Woods

In the forest, squirrels prance,
A dog thinks it's a dance.
Tree trunks hug, so stout and wide,
What secrets do they hide?

A raccoon steals a midnight snack,
While the owl gives a wise clack.
The bushes giggle, branches sway,
Oh, what fun they have at play!

A fox with tricks up its sleeve,
Tells tales most hard to believe.
While the trees lean in to hear,
Laughing loud, no need to fear.

The winds carry barks and howls,
As nature grins and loudly growls.
In this woods of whispered glee,
Even the shadows dance with me!

Prose from the Pooch's Perspective

Oh, what joy when I see a cat,
I chase it with a silly spat.
It climbs up high, I bark below,
'Come down!', I say, for fun, you know.

With sticks in tow, I roam about,
Sniffing here and checking out.
The humans laugh, they think it's sweet,
When I bound around on happy feet.

They toss the ball, I run like mad,
Bring it back? Oh, I feel glad!
But every time, I must admit,
I'd rather chew than fetch and sit!

A neighbor's dog gives me a wink,
Its owner thinks I'm on the brink.
But in my world, with sun and fun,
A pup's true life has just begun!

Sketches from the Street

On corners bright, the tale unfolds,
With pups and pals, our laughter holds.
A statue's pose looks quite absurd,
While chasing tails, we share few words.

The pigeons strut, all feathery gray,
But we just sniff and bark away.
As cars zoom by and humans stare,
We compose a song that fills the air.

A leash that's tangled, oh what fun!
Dodging puddles, we try to run.
With wiggly tails and floppy ears,
We're kings and queens of our frontiers.

The sun dips low, the shadows grow,
With every paw-step, memories flow.
On streets where laughter likes to meet,
Life's just a sketch, a goofy beat!

Canines in Contemplation

As I lie and ponder deep,
What dreams may come while I doze and sleep?
A bone banquet, or a chase with glee,
What's the best treat life could offer me?

The neighbor's cat looks rather coy,
Is it plotting something to annoy?
I wag my tail, unsure what to do,
Should I bark, pretend, or just pursue?

The trees sway gently, whisper hints,
In this moment, my heart does print.
I think of friends, both near and far,
Every wag a wish upon a star.

So I rest my head, the sun dips low,
Life's little puzzles, in whispers flow.
With dreams of treats and tails held high,
Tomorrow, oh tomorrow, we'll touch the sky!

Scribbles Over the Meadow

In a field of chaos, pens do dance,
Scribbles flying, giving words a chance.
With giggles erupting, the joy is clear,
Wild ideas wag, bringing fun year near.

A doodle here, a sketch over there,
Chasing butterflies, oh, what a flare!
The sun is shining, the ink flows free,
Join this frolic, come laugh with me!

With each stroke of whimsy, the colors blend,
A masterpiece born, waiting to mend.
The grass is alive with a scribbly cheer,
Let's write till the stars twinkle near!

And when dusk settles, the pencils tire,
We scribble our stories, a joyful choir.
In the meadow of laughter, we play and roam,
Every jotted jest feels just like home.

The Woof of Inspiration

In the park of ideas, dogs prance around,
Each wag a story, new tales abound.
With a bark of humor, they chase the day,
Inspiration howls, come join the fray!

With floppy ears, they listen so well,
To the whispers of dreams that we can tell.
A wagging tail shakes the cobwebs loose,
As goofy thoughts frolic, ready for use!

Nibbling at verses, they snatch a rhyme,
Each woof a prompt that echoes through time.
So grab a seat, watch these pups play,
They'll fetch the ideas that brighten the day!

As the sun sets low, and joy fills the air,
We gather the laughs that together we share.
The woof of our hearts will echo forever,
In the laughter we find, we're all clever!

Penning Between the Trees

Under the branches, pens take flight,
Ink flows like rivers, oh, what a sight!
Each leaf a canvas, a story to spin,
With giggles and grins, let the fun begin!

Scribbling secrets, the squirrels unite,
In a symphony of chaos, pure delight.
Each bark of a tree, a call to create,
Magical moments, where dreams can't wait!

With twigs as our brushes, we paint the sky,
On the pages of whimsy, together we fly.
The laughter of nature, the giggles of trees,
All join the chorus, carried on the breeze!

So let's pen our tales, in this forest of whim,
Where the branches of joy omnipresently brim.
Dancing through paragraphs, we twirl with glee,
Penning between the trees, just you and me!

Tail-Wagging Tales

Gather 'round friends, it's storytime here,
With tails a-wagging, we've nothing to fear.
From fluffy adventures, to bumpy rides,
Each tale is a treasure, where laughter resides!

Woofing with glee, the pups take the stage,
Unleashing their charms, we turn every page.
With knotted leashes and shoes askew,
Every laugh shared brings us closer, it's true!

A swish of a tail, a bark loud as thunder,
Spellbinding antics, we can't help but wonder.
Chasing the sun, bounding with cheer,
These tail-wagging tales bring us all near!

As stories sink in, dreamy pooches doze,
In a world full of giggles, imagination grows.
From whimsical barks to joyful frays,
We dance in this journey of tail-wagging ways!

The Creative Canine Call

In the park, the pups convene,
With minds like wags, they plot a scene.
A bark, a yip, they hustle and trot,
Paw-sitive vibes are what they've got.

A tail that wags, a nose that sniffs,
With every bark, they share their riffs.
Leashes tangled, they spin around,
In this funny realm, joy is abound.

They draft their tales on blades of grass,
A pup's best friend, it never will pass.
With doggy dreams and silly schemes,
Together they weave their fanciful themes.

When playtime ends, they gather near,
With howls of laughter, it's loud and clear.
They roll in joy, what a funny sight,
Canine creatives, all day and night.

Verses in the Verdant

In fields of green, the dogs do play,
Chasing echoes of words, come what may.
They bark out rhymes as they run,
Creating verses, all in good fun.

With floppy ears and silly grins,
They compose their tales, where laughter begins.
With every leap, a pun takes flight,
In the whimsical world, all feels just right.

They dig for ideas in soft, loose dirt,
With wagging tails, they share their heart.
A playful bark, a wagging cheer,
These furry poets spread joy far and near.

As daylight fades, they gather 'round,
Under moonlit skies, new tales abound.
In the glow of stars, their thoughts do blend,
Canine jesters, forever best friends.

A Journey with Paws and Pens

With paws like pens, they roam and write,
Chasing birds in the morning light.
Each wag a word, each bark a verse,
In their silly world, they intersperse.

On adventures grand, they wander near,
In laughter's embrace, there's nothing to fear.
They script a story with every chase,
With wet noses and boundless grace.

Through puddles and grass, they dance with flair,
With canine charms, they're a funny pair.
Each twist and turn brings giggles anew,
Their furry tails tell tales, that's true!

As day turns to dusk, the laughter stays,
With dreamy eyes, they share their ways.
In the pages of life, they leave their mark,
Paws and pens unite, igniting a spark.

Captured in Canine Cadence

In the rhythm of barks, a melody flows,
As dogs delineate life, with all its woes.
A woof here, a wag there, they strut with glee,
Creating a symphony, all wild and free.

With collars jingling, they prance in time,
Each step a beat, each bark a rhyme.
From playful spins to sneaky peeks,
Their joyful cadence is what everyone seeks.

They chase their tails in circles so round,
While giggling softly, joy does abound.
A silly leap, a puppy's frolic,
Their canine dance turns into a comic.

As daylight dims, their tales are spun,
In twilight's glow, the laughter's never done.
Bound by the cadence of life's funny play,
These pups make poetry in their own playful way.

The Howl of Written Worlds

In a forest of words, where tales do run,
A dog with a quill thinks writing's such fun.
Chasing after commas and sniffing at rhyme,
With barks as his editor, he keeps perfect time.

He paws at the pages with unexpected flair,
Giving prose a twist in the brisk morning air.
His tail wags in rhythm to every new line,
Creating a chaos that's simply divine.

Each bark is a chapter, each sniff a new plot,
With ideas a'howling, he scribbles a lot.
Under trees full of letters, so jovial and free,
This canine composer has visions to see.

So if you hear laughter from pages below,
It's the tale of a pup whose talent will grow.
With a howl and a yip, he's the star of the show,
In his whimsical world where the ink dares to flow.

The Scribe's Leafy Haven

In a garden of words, green leaves twist and twine,
Where scribbles with scribes are perfectly divine.
A leaf falls as a bookmark in nature's grand book,
While the writer just stops for a second to look.

The squirrels hold a meeting, the rabbits compose,
While the dog takes a nap, still dreaming of prose.
His paws make impressions where stories unfold,
In this leafy retreat where adventures are bold.

The quills and the paws dance around on the ground,
Creating a symphony, delightful, profound.
With each scratch and wag, the words come to life,
In this scribe's leafy haven, there's joy without strife.

Beneath branches of laughter, where tales find their home,
The writer's companion can magically roam.
With a bark and a wiggle, he deepens the lore,
In this hav'n of happiness, we always want more!

Echoes in the Scripted Grove

In the grove of ideas where echoes play tease,
Words flutter like leaves in the gentle spring breeze.
A dog eavesdrops on pages, a tail wagging bright,
As characters bicker from morning to night.

The rabbits are plotting their next daring heist,
While the dog scribbles notes on his mushroom-like tryst.
Excitement and laughter ring out through the air,
As adventures unfold with a whimsical flair.

Each bark adds a chapter, each tail wag a twist,
In this scripted grove, it's hard to resist.
With every new stanza, the forest does cheer,
As puns and poodles leap, making nonsense quite clear.

So join in the fun, bring your own clever quill,
In this echo-filled haven, let nonsense fulfill.
A playful reminder to write without fear,
In the scripted grove, there's just laughter and cheer!

Pencils and Pawprints

With pencils as swords and a notebook for a shield,
A puppy declares, "Let the words be revealed!"
He scampers through papers with glee in his stride,
While his pawprints dance wildly, nowhere to hide.

Each scribble is magic, each note tells a tale,
With fur all around, it's a furry detail.
He chases the grammar like butterflies' flight,
And nibbles on verses—a comical sight.

His favorite treat? A blank page to maul,
Pawprints and doodles are shared with us all.
With a bark and a scribble, he dreams up a spree,
In this land of creation, it's funny as can be.

So grab a soft pencil and join in the fun,
With tales by the pup, the laughter's just begun.
In a world full of words, let your joy never meet,
Where pencils and pawprints give magic a beat!

Littered Lines of Literature

A squirrel stole my plot today,
I chased it on my own old way.
My pen ran wild, a doggone spree,
But words unraveled, can't you see?

The cat thinks she can write a tome,
While I just chew on rhymes like bone.
With every bark, I draft a page,
Yet find myself lost in a cage.

My thoughts are tangled, like my leash,
Each idea wags, but never flees.
I'll fetch a story, make it bright,
With puns that make the moon take flight.

So here we are, a jumbled mess,
But who needs order? I must confess.
In chaos, we create delight,
A furry tale from day to night.

The Bark of Creativity

In the park, ideas run wild,
Each bellow a giggle, joyfully filed.
I bark at clouds, let my thoughts soar,
As bees buzz by, and I ask for more.

My pencil wiggles, like my tail,
Chasing down phrasing, a rhyming trail.
Sniffing out laughter, a fragrant breeze,
I carve out stories with belly-aching ease.

Woofs of whimsy ring out loud,
As I scratch my head, feeling proud.
I dig deep for humor, unearthing fun,
With silly twists that rattle and run.

So let's unleash our goofy tales,
In this writers' park, where madness prevails.
With every yip, creativity spins,
In the world of words, let the frolicking begin!

The Canine Chronicle

Gather 'round pups, the tale is set,
A legendary quest we won't forget.
With noses to the ground, we track our dream,
As laughter echoes, we're a funny team.

The mailman passes, oh what a sight!
Chasing our thoughts, we take off in flight.
Each bark a chapter, playful and bright,
In this canine saga, we own the night.

With wags and wiggles, our story spills,
In the backyard scribbles, we fetch the thrills.
A squirrel steals plot twists, how rude,
Yet we gather again, never deterred by mood.

Here's to our cronies, with humor and cheer,
In writing we trust, with friends ever near.
From leash to page, our voices combine,
In this lively chronicle, we wholly shine!

Unleashed Expressions

With a flip of the tail, ideas take flight,
I bounce and I pounce, all bubbling with might.
Each line is a chase, renewed every day,
As I scribble love notes in a comical way.

A tennis ball of thoughts bounces around,
Chasing wild verses that have yet to be found.
With giggles and grumbles, the stories resound,
In this furry fiesta, joy knows no bound.

Snouts in the air, we sniff for the fun,
With each silly bark, a new pun is spun.
So gather your treats, let's share a good laugh,
We'll write with our tails, on this creative path.

In the realm of the goofy, we'll leave a mark,
With unleashed expressions, a poetic spark.
So let the words wag, let the laughter flow,
In this canine caper, the fun will just grow!

Wags of the Whimsical

In a park where giggles play,
My dog thinks he's a ballet,
He twirls, he spins, with such grace,
Paw-tastic moves, a silly face.

With a sock tucked in his mouth,
He struts around, a rogue uncouth,
Neighbors laugh, they stop and stare,
He's the star with fluffy hair!

Rolling hills where laughter flows,
His tail a wag, as mischief grows,
Chasing butterflies, oh so sly,
He leaps and barks—oh my, oh my!

Each woof a giggle, each jump a cheer,
Furry comedian, spreading good cheer,
In his world of whimsy and fun,
Every day's a pun-filled run!

Wanderer's Reflections

A pup with dreams of distant lands,
Stomping through dirt with muddy paws,
Chasing tails, his own he expands,
Seeking adventure, breaking laws.

He stops to ponder, looks so profound,
Is that a squirrel? Or just a sound?
With a tilt of the head, he mulls and ponders,
In this wilderness, his mind wanders.

The sights he sees, the smells that thrill,
From garden gnomes to that climbing hill,
With every sniff, a tale unfolds,
Adventures in jest, forever told.

He meets the postman, gives a bright bark,
Their daily duel, a humorous lark,
In the world of wonders, so vast, so free,
Who knew a pup could hold such glee?

The Poet's Fetch

With a stick in mouth, he dashes away,
My faithful scribe, he's got much to say,
Between the barks and wag of his tail,
He's penning a tale that's sure not to fail.

He brings the ball like a golden prize,
Leaping and bounding with sparkling eyes,
In the poetry of paws, each wiggle's a word,
His furry verses are always heard.

The squirrels watch, bemused for a while,
As he spins in circles, oh what a style,
An author in fur, with bursts of delight,
Crafting his sonnets from morning till night.

Each frisbee catch, a stanza complete,
In my heart, he's both silly and sweet,
The poet's fetch is a wild affair,
In every wag, there's a story to share.

Fur-tales from the Frontline

In the trenches of my living room,
My brave explorer stirs from his gloom,
With paw prints left on history's page,
His quests are silly, full of rage.

The couch, a castle; the floor, a moat,
Every day's a war, on a rogue remote,
He sniffs out danger, with a playful bark,
In his furry mind, he's a fearless park.

With squeaky toys as his loyal team,
He battles dust bunnies, with zest and steam,
Charging forth like a knight in fur,
Against the vacuum's growl, he'll always stir.

So here's to the saga of fluff on patrol,
His laughter-filled missions take a toll,
From skirmishes with crumbs to heroic leaps,
Each hair-raising tale—my heart it keeps!

Echoes in the Enchanted Forest

In the forest, whispers play,
Squirrels gossip night and day.
Mushrooms dance, and owls hoot,
Even trees can twitch and scoot.

Frogs croak songs of rainy days,
While chipmunks plot their little ways.
Every branch has tales to tell,
Of secret mischief, oh so swell!

Leaves chuckle with a playful breeze,
The flowers wiggle, doing as they please.
Echoes bounce from bark to bark,
Laughter lighting up the dark.

As night descends, the creatures meet,
To share their snacks, oh what a treat!
In this land where joy is free,
Every tree hums a melody.

Rhyme of the Rover

A dog named Rover loved to rhyme,
He'd bark his verse at any time.
With every woof, he'd muse and play,
In wagging tails, ideas sway.

He'd rhyme with cats, and even mice,
Each line delivered, oh so nice!
Rover's rhymes brought giggles round,
In every corner of the town.

Chasing up a tail of dreams,
Life is better than it seems.
Rover's passion, pure delight,
Turns the day into a night.

With every bark, a lyric spins,
Dancin' paws and silly grins.
His joy in verse is plain to see,
In roam and rhyme, we're all so free!

A Bark in the Night

Underneath the moonlit sky,
A silly pup begins to try.
With a bark that shatters peace,
He thinks he's found a new release.

The owls hoot, the crickets sing,
While Rover dreams of playful spring.
A howling moon begins to glow,
He chases shadows, putting on a show.

With each echo down the lane,
He jumps and barks, again and again.
While neighbors laugh from beds so tight,
Thanks to that bark in the night!

Yet through the giggles and jeers,
This roving pup sparks all our cheers.
His nightly antics, pure delight,
With dreams of barks, and starry light!

Forest Fables and Fur

In a forest of fables, fur flies,
Where raccoons wear their funny ties.
Each tree tells a tale so rare,
Of misadventures floating in air.

Brave rabbits plot mischief at noon,
While hedgehogs dance to a fiddler's tune.
Every critter with laughter shared,
A story whirls, with fur unprepared.

The chipmunk's wisdom was a real delight,
As he pondered the moon and stars so bright.
With giggle fits, the beasts conspire,
In furry fables, they never tire.

So as they romp through woods of cheer,
Remember, laughter's always near.
Fables of fur with joy we spread,
In this forest where none feel dread!

Lyrical Leashed Adventures

In the park, a leash wraps tight,
A pup with dreams of flight.
Chasing squirrels and birds galore,
As if the world's a candy store.

A wagging tail, a joyful bark,
Each step's a dance, a little spark.
With tangled owners, what a sight,
In this silly, furry delight!

A ball, a stick, they fly and roll,
In this game, we lose control.
Laughter echoes, skies are blue,
Each mishap feels like déjà vu.

So here we frolic, dog and human,
Lost in fun, like jazz in a tune.
Every bark, a joyful cheer,
A leash, a laugh, the time is near!

Whispers Among the Willows

In the breeze, the branches sway,
As pups trot by, a merry ballet.
With tails that wag like secret whispers,
They chase the shadows, mischief shivers.

Among the willows, laughter sings,
With playful leaps and wild flings.
Roll in leaves, a furry whirl,
Life's a playground, watch them twirl!

A squirrel darts, a warning bark,
And off they go, leaving their mark.
Through mud and grass, they bound and race,
Dirt-covered snouts, a happy face.

So here they prance in wild delight,
In this haven of sheer sunlight.
A stage set for their canine show,
With every twist and turn they go!

Blurred Lines of the Daydreamer

In a daze, a pup will dream,
Of barking plots, and ice cream streams.
With eyes half-closed, they see the sights,
Like pizza trucks in starry nights.

Pawprints scatter, lines blurred and free,
A chase of thoughts, a wild decree.
Snoozing here beneath the tree,
What's next for a pup like me?

A sudden jolt, a sound or sniff,
Now awake with a wobbly lift.
Was that a frisbee thrown in air?
Oh no! Just another empty chair.

Life's a canvas, splashed with fur,
Each day a tale, an endless blur.
With silly thoughts and dreams so bright,
A napping pup feels pure delight!

Romantic Rovers: A Poetic Pursuit

Two little pups, in love's embrace,
Sharing bones in a secret place.
With wagging tails, hearts racing fast,
In this furry world, they're unsurpassed.

A moonlit stroll, paws side by side,
Chasing dreams, with joy and pride.
Puppy kisses, soft and sweet,
Every moment, their hearts compete.

In joyous barks, their love does bloom,
In playful chases, they find their room.
With silly prances, laughter rings,
Their bond a melody, fluttering wings.

So here they dance, a comedic duo,
In this game of love, they steal the show.
Two hearts, one leash, a beautiful sight,
In every wag, they find delight!

The Literary Lab

In a lab where words collide,
Puppies bark and authors bide.
Chasing tails of tales galore,
Each plot twist leaves us wanting more.

With pens as wands, they take to flight,
Chasing dreams by day and night.
Expecting treats for every rhyme,
Fetching lines, oh what a time!

When Shakespeare meets a golden retriever,
Plotting paws make stories cleaver.
From barking habits to literary zest,
This merry team knows how to jest.

So grab a leash and join the fun,
In this lab where words outrun.
With woofs and giggles, tales unfold,
In laughter, our fables are told.

Paw-sitive Reflections

In mirrors that reflect a tail,
Paw-some vibes will never fail.
Wagging tongues and silly stances,
Every bark ignites new chances.

From puddles splashed to sunsets bright,
Paws and puns take off in flight.
Chasing shadows, dreams in tow,
Reflecting joy in all we show.

With wagging hearts and silly grins,
We ponder life and how it spins.
From muddy paws to floppy ears,
Each moment echoes through the years.

So laugh aloud, let worries cease,
With paw-sitive vibes, we find our peace.
In every woof, there's wisdom keen,
In laughter's wake, we chase the dream.

Howl of the Heartfelt

A moonlit night, a playful bark,
We gather 'round to leave our mark.
Under stars, our stories wail,
With heartfelt howls, we tell the tale.

Each woof a rhythm, each howl a tune,
Bouncing bright beneath the moon.
Joyful spirits take to the air,
Our furry voices fill the square.

Oh, hearts unite in laughter's sound,
As paws and souls twirl 'round and 'round.
In every note, our love is clear,
Through silly songs, we spread the cheer.

So let us howl until the dawn,
In canine grooves, our worries gone.
With heartfelt lyrics, we embrace,
In this joyful howl, we find our place.

The Harmony of the Hound

In a park where laughter flows,
A symphony of barks and bows.
With tails that wag in perfect tune,
Canine choirs under the moon.

From woofs to howls, we sing along,
The harmony of hounds is strong.
Each bark a note, each leap a phrase,
In this canine concert, we all raise.

With frolicking paws, we dance about,
In joyful steps, we leap and shout.
Every jump a rhythm, every roll a cheer,
In unity, our friendship's clear.

So gather near, and let us play,
In this symphony, we find our way.
With hearts entwined, we'll sing all day,
In the harmony of pups at play.

Petals and Prose

In the garden I saw a cat,
With glasses perched, looking quite fat.
She scribbled notes with a twig in paw,
Claiming to write a memoir of the law.

Bees buzzed nearby, quite confused,
Wondering why they were being used.
For pollinating flowers, all day and night,
But now, they're in a poet's plight!

A snail joined in, with a shell so bright,
Wrote haikus under the moonlight.
Saying "slow and steady wins the race,"
Though speed in poetry is quite a disgrace!

And there by the roses, a dog laid low,
Dreaming of words like a Shakespeare show.
He barked at rhymes floating in the air,
Saying, "This stanza needs a little flair!"

The Narrative Nook

In a nook filled with tales of glee,
A rabbit wrote tales of how to be free.
With carrots as pencils and lettuce for ink,
He penned his adventures with time to think.

A squirrel swung by with a grin so wide,
"Is that a book or just your pride?"
He tossed a acorn in a playful jest,
"Let's call it a manual for being the best!"

They chuckled together, oh what a sight!
A dialogue flowing well into the night.
Till clouds rolled in, bringing a rain,
And pages got soggy, oh what a pain!

But they laughed it off, with a funny cheer,
"Just rewrite it all, the end is near!"
And so they did, under branches and leaves,
Creating stories that tickle and tease.

Chronicles of the Curious Canine

A dog named Max dreamed of being a star,
With a typewriter gifted from a friend, the bazaar.
He wrote of squirrels, chases, and bones,
Adventurous tales curled up on his own.

But every time he hit the keys,
A hairball sneezed through the autumn breeze.
His pages fluttered like leaves in the air,
Making him wonder if writing was fair.

Then came a cat, sleek as could be,
"Your tales are absurd, let me show thee!"
She sauntered and scribed with a flick of her tail,
Max barked in laughter, "Now that's quite the tale!"

With double the fun and a twist of fate,
Together they wrote till breakfast was late.
"Here's to us, the weirdest of pair!"
Living each day with stories to share!

Verses by the Woodland Stream

By the stream where the ducks like to float,
A frog leaped in, wearing a tiny coat.
His notebook splashed with every jump,
He thought of rhymes with a great big thump.

With wise old owls observing him write,
"Dear Frog, your style is quite a delight!"
They hooted and clapped, causing quite the scene,
As new verses bubbled up in between.

A beaver chimed in with a dam of dreams,
"Let's build a story that flows and beams!"
Together they crafted a tale, quite absurd,
Of ducks who thought they could speak a word.

As twilight fell, they wrapped up their show,
With giggles and glee in the evening glow.
Just funny little lines from a woodland team,
Spinning their magic by the sparkling stream!

The Howl of the Heart

In the quiet of the night, he screams,
With a face full of dreams and silly schemes.
Chasing shadows, he leaps with glee,
A howl so loud, it's a sight to see.

He thinks he's tough, a regal king,
But slips on the rug—a comedic fling.
His tail wags with a playful grin,
In this comedy, we all win.

Oh, the drama of fetching a stick,
He runs like the wind, but it's all just trick.
With a hop and a skip, he miscalculates,
Falling headfirst into bushy mates.

The moonlight catches his goofy pose,
With a twinkle in his eye, he strikes a pose.
In the moon's embrace, he howls once more,
A heart full of laughter, we all adore.

Fragments from the Furry

From the corner of the couch, a wiggle appears,
With a toy in his mouth, he conquers our fears.
Each squeak is a symphony, a comical show,
As he tumbles and rolls, putting on a glow.

With toy squirrels as foes, he launches a fight,
Pouncing and bounding with pure delight.
His battle cries echo, a call to the fun,
While we laugh at the chaos, he's nowhere to run.

His fluff drifts like snow, a fluffy parade,
In this war of the wits, he is never afraid.
A patchwork of giggles, this furry delight,
Writing our stories in the dim of the night.

So let's raise a toast to this fuzzy beast,
Whose antics and quirks never seem to cease.
With each little fragment, our hearts he will win,
In this humorous tale, the laughter begins.

Shadows of the Sleeping Hound

In the afternoon sun, he snores with glee,
A king in his castle, oh can't you see?
Paws twitching wildly in dreams far away,
Fighting fierce beasts, or maybe just play.

The shadows dance lightly around his soft fur,
While he grumbles and mumbles, a sleepy purr.
In his world of slumber, he'd run for a mile,
With a wag and a wiggle, then rest for a while.

He steals all the cushions, sprawled out with flair,
With a goofy dog grin, he relaxes with care.
Pawprints on the carpet, evidence of fun,
This hound's heart is golden, he's our number one.

When night falls around, he awakens with strife,
Searching for snacks, oh the joy of his life.
In shadows he dwells, with mirth made so grand,
The antics of sleeping hound, the best in the land.

Paw Prints on the Paper

Scribbles and doodles, a papered affair,
With paw prints smudged, creating a flare.
Each step a new story, with laughter to share,
As crayons become prey, scattered everywhere.

In a sea of fur, he leaves his great mark,
An artist of chaos, igniting a spark.
With a swish and a wag, he takes off on a spree,
Sketching tales of adventure, wild and free.

His nose paints the history of snack hunts and games,
While parchment bears witness to his woofy aims.
With each little dash, he claims his own space,
In a world where fun leads this furry race.

So grab all your pencils, let's create with delight,
With paw prints as symbols, we'll pen through the night.
The joy of our stories, our laughter, our cheer,
With each furry pawprint, let's write without fear.

The Writer's Pack

In a forest where the scribes convene,
A pup with a pen starts to preen.
His tail wags fast with each new line,
Chasing down sentences, feeling fine.

A squirrel critic with a twitchy nose,
Snaps at the words, sits to compose.
While the birds above sing stories neat,
A howling chorus makes the day sweet.

At the base of a tree, thoughts take flight,
Where laughter echoes into the night.
Each bark and each giggle shows the way,
To write like the beasts, come what may.

With notebooks spread under leafy sights,
Creativity dances in playful heights.
The pack's united, all writers at play,
Crafting their tales in a furry ballet.

Whispered Words from the Wild

In the hush of the woods, secrets arise,
A cat with a quill gazes up at the skies.
Her meows turn to whispers of fanciful lore,
While creatures outside just stop and explore.

The bunnies giggle, as if in a jest,
Gathering close to hear the best.
With each little tale, they bounce with glee,
A raucous retelling of wild reverie.

Upon knotted branches, where owls have dreams,
The words twist and twirl like moonlit beams.
A laugh echoes loud, among shadows and trees,
While the forest takes kindly to silliness, please.

So gather your wits, and pen down the fun,
In this vibrant place where the wild thoughts run.
With a wink and a grin, let your stories unfurl,
In the depths of the woods, where imaginations whirl.

Prose Amidst the Pines

Beneath tall pines, where the squirrels delight,
A fox tells the tales of the moonlit night.
With paws on a page, he scribbles away,
Creating a plot that's quirky and gay.

The winds play tricks with a flurry of leaves,
As a rabbit recounts what the night believes.
In bursts of laughter, ideas ignite,
Turning whispers of darkness into pure light.

Amidst the trees, the dialogue flows,
A watermelon dream that everyone knows.
With paper and paw, they brew up a storm,
In prose of the woods where ideas transform.

So if you're in search of a chosen verse,
Join in the fun, this playful universe.
From furry scribes, let your stories glide,
In the realm of the green, where thoughts coincide.

Messages in the Muzzle

A pup with a pencil and joy in his heart,
    Barks out ideas that leap and dart.
He sends little notes tied tight with a bow,
As critters convene for a show of the show.

The hedgehogs gather, with curiosity wide,
    To read all the messages sent with pride.
Each phrase is a giggle, each bark like a song,
In the world of the wild, where nonsense belongs.

With exclamations as bright as the sun,
    Every tale is a treasure, every pun is fun.
Through rain-soaked mornings or cloudy skies,
    The laughter of friends is the greatest prize.

So share all your thoughts, don't be shy to relay,
In the vibrant world where we play every day.
With joy in their hearts and dreams on the run,
    Each message a kiss, every story a pun.

Whiskers and Words

In a cozy nook, with a tail on the floor,
A cat scratches lines, but then falls with a snore.
The ink spills around, the ideas take flight,
As dogs chase their tails, what a comical sight!

Paws on the pages, they dance with delight,
A mishmash of letters, the words take a bite.
The paper gets wet from a drooly joy,
A woeful muse, our furry little boy.

The feline stares wisely, with one eye half-closed,
While the dog snorts a chuckle, the plot then exposed.
A tussle of puns, they roll on the floor,
Creating a tale that's meant to be more!

So bring on the humor, the charm, and the care,
For stories that wag and tickle the air.
With whiskers and words, let the fun ever flow,
In a world full of laughter, let the furballs glow!

The Poem Before the Paw

Before every bark, there's a whisper of wit,
Where cats pounce on phrases, with a jittery split.
A squirrel outside with a twitch and a tease,
Inspiration strikes, but oh, how it flees!

The paws tap the rhythm, a dance on the page,
As thoughts tumble forward, the furball's engage.
With a pause for reflection, the duo conspires,
A chaos of laughter, igniting their fires.

The paper's their canvas, it crinkles with glee,
As the cat hurls a pun, "You can't catch me!"
While the dog joins the chorus, adding a bark,
Together they whirl, igniting the spark.

Oh, the poem before the paw, a comedic delight,
With tales of mischief that dance in the night.
So let them be silly, let their antics unfold,
For laughter's the story that never gets old.

The Narrative Nest

In a nest of soft cushions, the story begins,
With a cat on the throne and a dog with his spins.
Each tail tells a tale, spins a yarn of delight,
While nibbling on biscuits, oh what a sight!

The plot thickens quickly like a gravy so warm,
As paws scramble high, stirring up quite a swarm.
With a flick of the whiskers, the words start to sway,
In a funny ballet, they tango and play.

Giggles erupt at the villain's sly plot,
For the dog is a prince and the cat is a bot.
A caper ensues through the pages we roam,
In the narrative nest, they've made it their home.

So let laughter unfurl like a feather that flies,
As the feathery friends conjure up their surprise.
Wit gently swirls as they weave through the quest,
In this tale of mishaps, they truly are blessed!

Paws and Prose

With paws on the keyboard, they craft a delight,
A woof and a meow, what a comical sight!
In their world of prose, every line takes a turn,
For laughter ignites, oh, the tales that they churn!

Fur fluffs and scribbles, ink stains their paws,
While the cat snags a word, oh the feline applause!
The dog chases thoughts with a wag and a grin,
Each sentence a treat, let the fun times begin!

With a woofy enthusiasm, they edit with flair,
As the cat swats the comma right out of the air.
Together they tumble through puns thick and fast,
Every bark and each whisper, a good time amassed.

With paws in the prose and hearts full of cheer,
They spin all their stories, through giggles and sneers.
In the end, it's a romp down imagination's lane,
Where laughter and love are the ultimate gain!

Scribbles in the Shadowy Grove

In the grove where scribbles play,
A pencil wags, gone astray.
The trees giggle, leaves in dance,
As words take flight, a merry chance.

A raccoon dons a writer's cap,
He types away, but then a nap!
His paw slips down, a mess untold,
And rhymes turn silly, bright and bold.

Woofs of Wisdom

A trusty dog with wisdom old,
Barks advice worth more than gold.
"Heed the scratch upon your page,
A plot twist waits, release your cage!"

With every woof, a lesson shared,
In playful barks, our thoughts declared.
He rolls in ink, becoming muse,
A wagging tail, no chance to snooze!

The Writer's Best Friend

A loyal pup, with fur so bright,
Sits by my side, a true delight.
With every bark, he stirs my mind,
A partner in crime, of the funniest kind.

He fetches dreams, I toss the rhyme,
With each adventure, we waste no time.
Paw prints on pages, joyful and free,
This goofy pooch writes poetry with glee.

Chasing Words in the Wilderness

In the wild, where squirrels tease,
Words scatter like leaves in the breeze.
A pup bounds forth with a wagging tail,
Chasing phrases, he follows the trail.

Through thickets thick, they dart and dive,
"Come back, oh words, let's come alive!"
With every bark, a vibrant cheer,
The wilderness laughs, as fun draws near.

Scribbled Paw Prints

In the yard, a quest begins,
With floppy ears and toothy grins,
Chasing tails and wild dreams,
After words, it seems.

Paws on paper, scribbles flow,
The dog thinks it's a show,
Each bark a word, a riddle,
While humans chuckle, it's not middle.

Grass stains and ink collide,
With each paw print, they take pride,
The dog's tale is full of glee,
Happy tales for you and me.

Underneath the shade so wide,
A pup's imagination cannot hide,
Adventure waits in every line,
With furry friends, it's all divine!

The Fictional Fetch

A stick is tossed, the tale begins,
With epic quests and playful sins,
The dog leaps high, a noble knight,
To fetch the words in pure delight.

Mighty barks echo through the air,
As characters chase without a care,
Each tug a twist, a plot defined,
In the world of make-believe, they're lined.

Chew the scenery, take a break,
For every bone, a new mistake,
But laughter reigns, no need for stress,
In this fiction, we're truly blessed.

A wagging tail, a bouncing rhyme,
In this saga, we're lost in time,
With every fetch, let joy adhere,
As we spin tales of fun and cheer!

Howl of the Imagination

Under the stars, with moonlit glow,
A howling pup begins the show,
Tales of mischief, adventure and play,
Where wild imagination holds sway.

Spinning yarns of daring deeds,
The dog, a hero, follows its leads,
Each bark a chapter, loud and clear,
As audience chuckles, 'Oh, dear!'

Through fields of dreams, they laugh and leap,
Paw printed stories, forever to keep,
With every howl, new joys galore,
As tails wag wildly, who could ask for more?

A flick of the ear, a playful stare,
In this whimsical world, we declare,
Imagination runs wild and free,
With our furry friends, in harmony.

Realm of the Storyteller

In a cozy nook, tales abound,
With a wagging tail and joyful sound,
Every bark unlocks a door,
To worlds where laughter's never a bore.

The storyteller's paws tap away,
Creating mischief come what may,
Chasing lines as the pages turn,
For silly tales, our hearts do yearn.

A twist of fate, a furry plot,
In this realm, we find our spot,
Sniffing out the humor's scent,
With every tail, joy's heaven-sent.

So gather 'round for tales so bright,
As pups weave stories through the night,
In the realm where fun's the goal,
Together we share, we joyfully roll!

The Writer's Woodland Wander

In the woods where ideas play,
A squirrel steals my pen today.
I chase him round with joyful glee,
He writes a novel, just not for me.

The owls hoot in poetic tones,
Inspiring me with their wise groans.
A rabbit hops with rhythm in stride,
I laugh as he becomes my guide.

Each tree stands tall, with quirks to share,
One even sports a hat and stare.
The leaves burst forth like rhymes galore,
In this wood, I could write forevermore.

As dusk settles, my muse retreats,
Leaving behind some tasty treats.
I'll hang my thoughts upon a branch,
In this forest, I'll take my chance.

Rhyme Roots and Rhythm Branches

Underneath the boughs so wide,
Words wiggle in a playful slide.
With each step, a stanza unfolds,
The forest sings, its secrets told.

A raccoon drums with borrowed sticks,
As butterflies join in the mix.
They flit and flutter, curiously keen,
In this strange realm, they reign supreme.

I scribble notes upon the greens,
With wonder filling all my scenes.
The rhyme roots dig deep in the earth,
Each line a blossom, each word a birth.

The branches dance, they twist and twirl,
As laughter falls in a joyous whirl.
In this verdant kingdom, dreams align,
Where rhymes and roots forever intertwine.

Barking Words in the Lyrical Woods

In the thicket, words take flight,
A barking dog joins in the sight.
He howls a tune, so wild and free,
His barks beat time, a symphony.

The ferns are swaying, feeling bold,
As stories spill, a treasure untold.
With each step, my laughter bounces,
A bear nearby, it also flounces.

As afternoon sends shadows long,
I find my rhythm, I hum a song.
A vixen laughs, joins in my cheer,
With such companions, there's nothing to fear.

Even the rocks seem to dance with joy,
In this wording wood, I'm just a boy.
An endless script beneath the trees,
Where laughter echoes and worries ease.

Canine Companionship in Composition

With my pup, we roam the trails,
Each bark and wag, our laughter sails.
He digs for words, quite out of sight,
While I try penning through the night.

His tail is wagging, a metered beat,
As butterflies circle our little seat.
Together we craft tales quite bizarre,
In this cozy nook beneath the stars.

His paws dance lightly upon the page,
Doggy muses at a tender age.
We scribble tales of thrilling chases,
And epic quests in far-off places.

With canine charm and playful schemes,
We spin our fables, weave our dreams.
In this partnership of verse and bark,
Our story ignites like a bright, warm spark.

www.ingramcontent.com/pod-product-compliance
Lightning Source LLC
Chambersburg PA
CBHW072146200426
43209CB00051B/752